People in the Community

Teachers

Diyan Leake

Heinemann
LIBRARY

www.heinemann.co.uk/library
Visit our website to find out more information about Heinemann Library books.

To order:
☎ Phone 44 (0) 1865 888066
🖷 Send a fax to 44 (0) 1865 314091
🖥 Visit the Heinemann Bookshop at www.heinemann.co.uk/library to browse our catalogue and order online.

First published in Great Britain by Heinemann Library, Halley Court, Jordan Hill, Oxford OX2 8EJ, part of Pearson Education. Heinemann is a registered trademark of Pearson Education Ltd.

Editorial: Diyan Leake and Catherine Clarke
Design: Joanna Hinton-Malivoire and Steve Mead
Picture research: Tracy Cummins and Heather Maudlin
Production: Alison Parsons

Origination: Chroma Graphics (Overseas) Pte Ltd
Printed and bound in China by South China Printing Company Ltd

ISBN 978 0 431 19246 8
12 11 10 09 08
10 9 8 7 6 5 4 3 2 1

British Library Cataloguing in Publication Data
Leake, Diyan
Teachers. - (People in the community)
371.1
A full catalogue record for this book is available from the British Library.

Acknowledgments
The publishers would like to thank the following for permission to reproduce photographs:
©Age Fotostock pp. **9** (Stewart Cohen/Pam Ost), **16** (Jeff Greenberg); ©Alamy (Gapys Krzysztof) p. **12**; ©AP Photo (Tomas Munita) p. **15**; ©Corbis (Sophie Elbaz/Sygma) p. **20**; ©Getty Images pp. **4** (Fraser Hall), **5** (Amanda Hall), **6** (Paula Bronstein), **7** (Mustafa Ozer/AFP), **8** (Angelo Cavalli), **11** (Tony Metaxas), **13** (Rana Faure), **14** (T-Pool), **21** (China Photos), **22 (top)** (Rana Faure), **22 (middle)** (Fraser Hall), **22 (bottom)** (T-Pool); ©The Image Works (Arnold Gold/New Haven Register) p. **19**; ©Landov (Oswaldo Rivas/Reuters) p. **17**; ©Peter Arnold Inc. (Shehzad Noorani) p. **10**; ©PhotoEdit (Michael Newman) p. **18**.

Front cover photograph of a young boy counting dice at the Bohula Model Government Primary School in Habiganj Upazila in Sylhet District, Bangladesh, reproduced with permission of ©Peter Arnold Inc. (Shehzad Noorani). Back cover photograph reproduced with permission of ©Getty Images (Angelo Cavalli).

Every effort has been made to contact copyright holders of any material reproduced in this book. Any omissions will be rectified in subsequent printings if notice is given to the publisher.

Contents

Communities

People live in communities. They live near each other and help each other.

People work together in a community.

Teachers in the community

Teachers work in communities.

Teachers help people learn.

What teachers do

Teachers teach children.

Teachers teach adults.

Teachers teach reading and writing.

Teachers teach maths and science.

Where teachers work

Teachers work in schools.

Teachers work in colleges.

What teachers use

Teachers use whiteboards.

Teachers use books.

People who work with teachers

Teachers work with head teachers.

Teachers work with teaching assistants.

Teachers work with parents.

Teachers work with caretakers.

How teachers help us

Teachers help us learn.

Teachers help the community.

Picture glossary

 **college** place where adults go to learn

 **community** group of people living and working in the same area

 **whiteboard** board that teachers write on

Index

Notes for parents and teachers

This series introduces readers to the lives of different community workers, and explains some of the jobs they perform around the world. Some of the locations featured in this book include Cape Cod, USA (page 4); Ladakh, India (page 6); Habiganj Upazila, Bangladesh (page 10); Odessa, Ukraine (page 12); Ziarat Gali, Pakistan (page 15); Managua, Nicaragua (page 17); and Shigatse, China (page 21).

Before reading
Talk to the children about the work of a teacher. What do they think a teacher does? What would be the best thing about being a teacher? What would be the most difficult thing about being a teacher?

After reading
• Set up the role play area as a classroom. Place toys on chairs as pupils. Let children choose what they would like to teach. If possible, let them use a board to demonstrate their teaching.
• Sing this song to the tune of "If you're happy and you know it":
If you want to learn to read ask a teacher. (x2) If you want to learn to read you'll learn everything you need. If you want to learn to read ask a teacher. If you want to learn to add you don't need to feel sad.
• Play "Teacher Says" (based on "Simon Says"). Say: *Teacher says* (and give children a range of actions to follow). Then just say: *Do this.* Any child who performs the action is "out".